MUZZLE THYSELF

poems by

Lauren Fairbanks

Dalkey Archive Press

Dalkey Archive Press
Fairchild Hall / ISU
Normal, IL 61761
(309) 438-7555

Some of these poems have appeared in the *Literary Review* and *Another Chicago Magazine*.

Library of Congress Cataloging in Publication Data
Fairbanks, Lauren, 1958-
  Muzzle Thyself / Lauren Fairbanks
  I. Title.
PS3556.A3618M89 1991   811'.54—dc20   90-14058
ISBN: 0-916583-74-0

First Edition

Partially funded by grants from The National Endowment for the Arts and The Illinois Arts Council.

Dalkey Archive Press
1817 North 79th Avenue
Elmwood Park, IL 60635 USA

Printed on permanent/durable acid-free paper and bound in the United States of America.

To
Gilbert Sorrentino

Contents

We hate a man who continually promises to visit us and never does, but we invite him again to come and see us because we are excitable and nervous.

—Edward Dahlberg, *Reasons of the Heart*

Three Born in an Age

Sockless Einstein marched
in carpet slippers.
How sweet.
Twisting his hat
all the way
to the podium.
Tuck it in old man. Your shirt.
Al.
Al baby.
Twists his hat with bellhop charm.

Folks. What is blessed wrong?
Clock-wrongness in a
clock-right world.
Phallic things happen.
Take this ray.
(Ray accepted by audience.)

How did they wheel this guy in
from the beach?

A Rap with William Carlos Williams
We can't forget the picayune

W.C.W. Yoo Hoo. Little girl.
Did you want a little
bit about your Dad
where the protagonist
"sparrows," "I did my best;
FAREWELL," then clucks
off?
You DID [*laughs*]
want something to that
effect?

LITTLENESS? ASK THE
LIGHT AND MIRROR PEOPLE.

NOT SO LITTLE girl
chirped: Man mirrored
to me
STABBED
with sulphured hemlock
RIGHT EARS
while grudge-covetous
mudslung
Ma Bell flock
shot same
earful.
DIG THE YELLOW CONVENIENCE
OF SLUNG-DRUNK
MISREMEMBERING.

W.C.W. [*laughs*] AND THE YELLOW? [*laughs*]

NOT SO LITTLE girl
chirped: Cleanest happiness.
Smuttiest pain.
Flashing
protective yellow
is a ruffling tactic.
YELLOW
solidifies
listening right sides

where
silly little gals
are
OTHER men's daughters.
Clucking off
one will have a
reflexive need
to chirp
"I did my best . . ."

Mistaker

Select a DEVOTED TO THE LEADER
disciple.
Family Tie-offs. Blue-contact-lensed
outsiders
join the master race with peroxide.

A niche for you
on my high gothic ceiling.
Batlike, pop yourself up.

Don't breed with your own. DONATE.
Live Celibate in Celebes. DONATE.
Take Bromo Seltzer and breed with the Brombergs of Breton.
DONATE.

THINKING was your third PUSHINGUPDAISIES mistake.

She Poet

MURDERS paper
singing
"Bringing in the Sheaves."
FINDS poetry crawled inside
her ratty fox fur
where the hard shell fell
to ink-stained bedsheets.
White White White.
History was becoming the place to be.

WON'T HIDE "the danger"
in polyester petticoats.
IS a man.
GOES HUNTING.
Like a walrus,
tonsorially AFFECTS
long naval trailers.
IS weary of the hunt.
TAKES to the corner.
Mentally, HAS an outsize penis.
IS like fuchsia
like over there
behind the brain.
REMAINS seated
on her black leather trench.
AWAITS
the great unwashed.

LOVES it kamikaze.
NAPALMS with salt,
her pork.
WAS a country girl
in a doorway with a
fullup jug.
ERASES Scarlet Bignonia's
dance card.
NAPALMS with cayenne,
her pork.
STUFFS marbles fantastical and
marbles literal
into pockets.
FINDS words to replace

"feminine danger"
(Where's the bog?)

SHE POET
IS
the Gilda Gravy.

Songbirds are crunchy little appetizers.
The four nails of a passion were
significantly
four carrots in various stages of
decomposition.
Frosty cool light chilled me
and phosphorescent Jesus
became composure
himself.

West on Winged Drink

Unless we flatten all Latins
my Dago
will Alfa-Romeo
wine
and make a station of me.

Limey has me monthly
for geographical instruction.
Tea will be
POURED OUT.
I bring the biscuits.

Soul-seared-forested
Irish Catholics
have feet exposed.
You know they
can't drink a LITTLE.
They
go west on winged drink.

Boy Fronts Tank in T. Square
Encirclements of Phaedrus the Wolf

TOLD
>Do your door-to-door search for
>"the good."

TOLD
>Until noses blew like Paris
>squeaky beeps.

TOLD
>Dismiss a thought. Let on you're
>vixed.

TOLD
>On Costa Rican cattle ranchers.

WHO TOLD
>On Argentinean cattle ranchers.
>(Meat and blood's my motto too.)

PRAY FOR SUNSHINE WITHOUT MIRRORS
COMBINE WITH RUMORS OF MY BEING

TOLD.

Psssst. He'll not be needing to
surface near-naked in nude goatskin
shoes. Wolves define themselves in
brief high-pitched electronic signals.
Hear 'em?

After the big one,
life's walking in goatskin
round the smog-filled cemetery.

(Rear projection of natural sun
before the last scene.)

Ezra

Unmindful slut.
You make the freest hand seem covetous.
Eyes like the grey of the pounding sea.
Rot in lone womanish peace.

Listening.
I'm the listening mouth agape audience
listening
to the impurest story ever.
Hear slammer noises?
Just?
The Marquis' brain ripening in the shade.   SHADE OF
WHAT?
Blisters his brain into shape.   SHAPE OF?

Shape of slammer noises.
Mes amis were jailbirds.

MMBJ

He's shoes on my feet.
He's food in my belly.

Sometimes
when he's gone
I find myself
shoeless,
stinking and famished.

Bright ships left you this or that in fee
The wind rakes across my face
scraping orifice
encroachment impending
rakes down like chills
heavy wet breeze rakes a face
scraping
not a breeze
like chills
impending encroachment rakes up flesh
stop being an unmoored boat
in a weighted wet breeze
It rakes my face
scraping
Someone weighed the wet breeze
He had full sail beauty
Encroachment
iced pulse
Encroacher-raker
A soggy wind bludgeons my face and yours
ice pulse
Scrapes

Spicer Ropes

COMING AT AN END.
TO A FRAYED END.
STILL EXHAUSTED LOVERS
SINCE 1958.
JOININGS AND PARTINGS.
ONE LENGTH
OF COILED YELLOW PLASTIC ROPE.
MIDDLECOILING.

WOUNDROUND. UNDONE.
Straw's up short.
At the end of my spice.
Where love ends
like a rope.
Again.

Which Leaves Us with the Prioress

With or without
penchants for lips and meat pies,
bitching slits are a BITCH.
Triangles within ourselves.
Stripped slits on the head of a screw
cross each other up.

Locomotives sprout violets.
Trudie,
Luckless,
Hester,
and Prioress,
check each other's A's.
MINE'S BIGGEST.

P.R.E.T.T.Y. THINKING TRUDIE SINGLE "BEYOND HER FIRST
    YOUTH."
P.R.E.T.T.Y. THINKING LUCKLESS A WOMAN "OF A CERTAIN
    AGE."

Silken scab lines prevent Luckless slit beheadings.
Prioress dusts plastic technicolor lips.
Bitching slits are a BITCH.

While mad, pious, and keeping herself steady Co.,
VERMILION is Hester's (bitching slit) emotion.

Professional java-slinging Wanda promises
to be more than mentally gone
with child.
The color of a dimple-kneed rose fades.
A face painted with kohl is the extent
of her creative abilities.
The extent of his.

Magazines devoted to jugs
show black holes in place of extremities.

Fashion,
since Hector unleashed himself,
is butchered pain,
is extremities burned full off.

On gaudy nights
a scrubbed brain
is a giddy child
is a muddled brain
such gaudy nights.

Platinum blondes
locquaciously grapple
with placenta.

Starlet knees
gently touching
thrust
through
silken nights.
Gaudy Nights.

Neo-Pagan Baby in Surfer Neon

Son of a Scandinavian
wasn't a lifeguard.
Begged me
not to
PLEASE
insult him.
Neobohemianconman.
CRISP.
One hands in one's machete.

A neobohemian
in black lipstick
myself once.

Get your own crisp to leper
sunburn.
My love is bigger than a skateboard.
It's a crisp start.
Two born casualties
constitute a takeover
on Nazi turf.

A hole is drilled in this part of your soul.
To-waist your hair.
YOUR BAT.
Go in peace.
You're entitled to
entitle yourself
NITROGEN-RICH BUG.

I: Mamma Buzzard at
the Workhouse on Grand Larceny

Have the men did
Si Si Fixabelle wrong?
Fun to live with three
strays
were brought home
to amuse
(FLOATS OVER THE LAND — AMUSE A SHUT-IN)
unradiated.
Tends to amuse
Si Si Fixabelle.

Three
of us that gangrened day.
Home builds itself
on pillars of salt.
Si Si's cowtown wish:
Stop being a them what's talk
about it and become a
them what's
do.
Si Si
crewcut clipped
her words.

Noise in the stacks is only
nobody;
cashmere-ragged SMARTshirts
impressing themselves.
Goddesses don't flinch.
Goddesses
have no problem getting ribbons
from snakesnarls.
Windshields are checkered pasts.

She whispered
TOO MUCH WINDBLOWN TALENT
to a "not our crowd"
table. Good blokes talk
"Ringstrasse, Vienna's . . ."

II: Mamma Buzzard, FOND of Pineapple Patch Prison

Si Si's a gentleman's daughter,
praying in mauve-lipped seriousness.
Serious as electroplated
forks,
as dining is
bacon grease dining.
as . . .

The fun to live with three
dine badly.
Minutes deepen
to catch a drift.
Three spit to wasted dyings.
"ALWAYS SOME DAME.
PROFESSIONAL . . ."
(buyer of old-hat clothes.)

Buzzard brothers watch Si Si
STICK EMOTIONS ON
visits to the urinal.

Three of us
repaired ourselves to the
bar
TO FACILITATE THE UNSMEARING
of clarity.

Si Si Fixabelle, no longer
prideful,
is familiar with the color
red. It's colorful.
Comes in armfuls.

Splitting Heirs

Delila is the
bluetuturelieved girl
always married
never dating.
SIMSON AND DELILA 1902
HANGS IN THE
"Boil a Monarch Doll Co."
atrium.

Two hungry ones are mattressed
in a sparse room.
Bedflung unregal flashers
avoid Vietnam electronics.
HUNGRY make nests of long hairs.
Brriinnnggg.
Answering machines
are stacked.

Delila waves detached locks
bellyaching
IF EACH DOLL PULLED ONE HAIR . . .
The wave is to invisible voyeurs
D. squawks GOTTA PIECE A' TUBA HERE
WHERE A MAN USED TO BE.

He mattresses her
in a sparse room.
Holds a splayed leg.
Brriinnngggsss
whether or not
Simson is home.

A Snuggle About-face Life

Chemical dandyism. Our
bodyheat problem.

Violent exception
taken to us.

Same bare malfunctioning
engine escape.

Blooded orifice
Clotting factors
Squirming Catholics
Cauterize
Tourniquet
Quit
Kiss and make up.
Easy target styles
razed to the . . .

Owner of my handkerchief
BLOWS.
Bumvivant
switches
name-brand snot rags.

Screwpress
my twisted bandage
about-face.
Be
my red-gobbed
Polish lancer.

Gawking with Intent to Commit Mopery

Door open.
Oh. It's you.
Wee hours holder.
M.O.P.E.
expected.

Being bad's his way
of leaving.
Goes as Piñata.
As pained dignity.
Erect
as dependable
erectile tissue.

All wet
wise as the spring
as one
once again
moves toward
wet.
Waits
and is no orange twig.

Feels Like a Real Fight
(Ted and Steve)

BEFORE
THEY COULD PETRIFY
TO WOODEN PLANKS
YOUR DAD
A FORTIFIED TOWN
BESTOWED WITH
THE POWERS OF FISHING
DREW
THE SPECKS FROM EACH OF YOUR EYES.

WITH MUSCULAR BRUSHSTROKE
TRACED SHUDDERS,
SENT SHUDDERS
TO SAME WINDS OF ACQUAINTANCE.

THE REAL FIGHT
IS UNFORTIFIED
BY SHATTERED WINDS
OF ACQUAINTANCE.

HINDWARD
DEATHBOUND
HE JUMPS A RATTLING
AMERICAN HIGHWAY TRUCK
FAST
HARD
FAR INTO THE TUNNEL
WHERE BACKSTAIRS INFLUENCE
IS THE WHITE MAN'S
TIME-SPRATTERED AGONY.

BRUSHLOST BRISTLES
SPRATTER AND SPREAD TO WINDS
OF QUESTIONABLE ACQUAINTANCE.

A GOOD MAN
STILL rips out young buck's
door handles.
STILL jumps living room grenades
and kitchen couches it
in the jacked-up part of what's
STILL
Thank God
A REAL FIGHT.

Harridans Harridans Harridans Harridans

Her wake up tendency.
Bowling ball face.
Charlie Brown head.
Cereal dead ass.
Tendency to make
RASPUTIN WAS HERE
shirts.

It's female
It's vicarious.

MATURE
wait in line muttering
mine mine mine mine
YOURS.
Watch them take it
THOUGHT IT WAS MINE . . .
away.
All belongs to the skinny one
carving initials
screaming
YOURS.

Difference in a Florida bag lady
is the bicycle,
is
double coolers on her rack.

Florida

I once knew a man who came back
ink-kneed
more than twice
Let me tell you he's terrific.
Four-day tattoos wear off.
Savaging whole lobsters . . .
Calling dark and red . . .
Calling stampeding dread and sore waves of ecstasy . . .
Sore waves of ecstasy.

Laughs at my whittlings
My weigh station with words
Worries it out.

Up in sailofts
bogbodies give birth to a wind machine.

Thought this engine room of the northeast
a leisure park valley of smudge and cinder.
Sledgehammer daughters are industrial art.
Sledgehammer daughter AM industrial art.

Now I walk dark
tinswelling
and a ways behind myself.

This or that under glass comes to that.
Under glass.

Writing sideways
wearing kissproof lipstick
writing that
stampeding dread's from eating coffe with a fork.
Coffee with one *e*.

This or that under glass comes to that
Under glass.

In Jean Arthur's Voice:
We Making Gelt Yet?

To camp
was to carp
was to return tap-dancing sycophants
to the stage.
RID HERSELF OF THE GUY
                   CALLED IT SHARING. HEX HER HOPEFUL.
REDGLASSED. Redglassed city girls.
And the city laughs.
Golden radiance is a bore. We saving $ yet?
Misplaced feminine mystique
is a (Styled himself "a prince")
muscle
is a
smells of coconut meat
rump.

Ambidex
instructor at misremembering
"Sluggy"
snorts coral Peruvian flakes.
Picks pieces of conch
from tresses.

A knife.
A fork.
No. It's eyeglasses.
Rip the platinum and pig iron
arrows of misfortune from her lapel.
Fuck an eye out.
She'll only have three.

Name your
hex her hopeful
utensil.

ARE WE
As Beatle Boots phase moves to
pointy Armani shoes phase.
MAKING $
YET?

How Many Frenchmen Before I'm Wrong?
I'm Wrong!

YOU.
ONLY.
Could motivate me to a night office.
CRISP. TWENTIES. Restore fug and gloom.

Seeing red warms
Eyes
warm
are variations on pink eye.

Bald chick hairdo
does you for me.

Wish is for one of your five o'clock shadows.
Fast as a one-block cab ride;
affiliate with me long as ass-available
is the cutest.

IRISH.   IN YOUR ALLEY.   CAT.

A SHE IS   UNDERESTIMATED FANTASY.
A SHE IS   LARGE AND WOODEN.
A SHE IS   A DIFFERENT WHITENESS TO A WALL.

CRISP.
Little brother

Little
        little brother.

Fingers press to nothing discussed.
Cypress spires root me in fingers press.

IF YOUR MOTHER WASN'T ALWAYS CALLING YOU ...
I'd say EVERYBODY;
You and Spic and Span (Two Irish
Vaudevillians)
on three takes,
is taken to the cleaners.

The guy always comes up smelling like
a sandalwood elephant.
It troubles me
It troubles me
It troubles . . .
He troubles me.

Truism for our cities
of great unwashed populations:
nothing succeeds like excess.
Economically and chemically
depressed
peoples
leave
chunks of digital time
on my hands.

Bought a sky scope at PINOCCHIO.
They think I'm looking into my pen.
It's my sky scope.
So. I'm a little weird.

They say
long-nosed liars
with black-spotted tongues
congregate under wood-carving tools
which facilitate spindle-turning.

The sordid will have spotted
the sexual allusion.

A LOTTA LOTTA WEIRD, I heard you say.

One Yang Child

Occidentalized,
she wears mythological dishpan metals.
IS a braceletted pagan
BAKING.

IS a smell ground in India
IS clear carnelian daughter
to his mother bead.

Sea grape on
ho
what a grapevine.
In. Just. Otherfresh.

Dead eyes are diamondependent
rivals
flexing to muscle memory.
To Yin is to Yang
is a brick house.

Copper creation folks
dig on carnelian.
So I pop myself
down from my
cross
and say
YOU
SHOD LIKE A PRINCESS,
COPPERCOLORED SMARTBUTT,
T'AIN'T TOO MUCH
FOR ONE YANG CHILD TO LUMP.

Little Willie Blowin'
Chicago-style BLUES To-nite

Carnival ringmaster insta-flashes
for posterity.
Posterity
hikes anniversary skirts in the Cinnamon Room.
To-nite.
Maybe so. Maybe so.
Audience of blowers.
Bouncer/waiter in red nylon V-neck
wants $2.25 for a club soda and what? lime.
                and what? lime.
                and what? LEMON.

ALL ABOUT TENSION AND RELEASE.
"Do it white boy"
finds himself
"in the pocket." Maybe so. Maybe so.

Little Willie down DOWN
"spite a' fruicky bass playin"
down
Down
DOWN TO . . . MAYBE SO. Maybe so.
DOWN
on
echo
amp'd in Marine Band Harp.

FOLKS STILL THROW $$$$$$$$?
You just seen it.
Maybe so,
maybe
so.

Carpe Diem

THE CITIZEN has ambrosial locks. GOLD IS A
METAL.
Full-bosomed girls promenade.
Takes it in while I look
THE PAPERBOY.
Chest sinking
sinks to concave.
Nestle in this
lap of cushy comfort.

You and me could really exist
I speculated.
EXIST
dying piecemeal.

How GOOD is the brilliant but
lazy one?
BRILLIANT. LAZY.
Who shall I say is inquiring?
Trying to live before we die is my answer.

Our CITIZEN,
a festivity-sparked burning particle
runs to the crowded room,
befriends magic,
runs with it.
"Urchin,"
buzzes magical incantations
racing
to catch the bee woman's strings.
RACING. Stops intermittently.
Plops to handstand.
CORRECTLY
ABERRANT
HANDSTANDING
IS INCLUDED IN TONITE'S PROGRAM.

His honeystuck fingers are axle-greased
tools
are callused brains.

She-snob robs the altar,
chomps the bony sacrifice
with worn cuspids mouthing,
TOOLBOX SMELLS ARE DEEP AND DIRTY.

CITIZEN! MURDER AND CREATE.
drybrained in a wet season, yours
is a liquid glory when the monsoons come.

Who's Wallowing?

Touch the knobby pearls.
Fold into sand
mud
of my mud
you are the first
you are the last mud
Folding.

Dear Bitch

She happened upon a love "so polite."
Only damned limey in all Oregon.
I'll take the post.
It's an honorary chair.
"Concubinus in Exile."
I'm pending. To be Willie Mays or not.
I am
the cracked
and exiled (to Mom's)
recipient of a one-way barge transfer
and Dear John pink slip.

Dear John.

Slow talkin' mystic ways.
Playful walkin' fleshy limbed
mystic ways.

Complain ski-hatted
eagle-beaked mope.
Don't ever change. CHANGE.
Don't ever change. CHANGE.

Hellos strangers in the loop.
Gat-toothed taboo
to Saturday
moments before Christmas
DO.

The last time
I donate my senses to a charitable
fly-by-night
foundation.
If ever a mango got a hold . . .

The phase of finding myself
particularly dead without him.

Like any rock slung chance to pass,
this too shall pass.

Knobs adjusted on café noir blood.

Like any rock slung chance to pass . . .

Un Garçon Mal Pensant

Forever and forever and forever.
You expect beauties to be smart? ASS.
Throw her OFF.
Stupid ASS JERK.

The blackhaired grudgholding thing
STRADDLES YOU
Forever and Forever and Forever.
DENY YOUR ASPIRATION TO MAKE A NEST OF HER!

Noisome monkeys
needlessly
make sorrowful noises overhead.

Far as arms
arms as seats of love
can throw
for a loop.

My curse:
SHE SHALL NOT FIND SILKEN STREAMERS
EXTENDING FOREVER AND FOREVER
BUT A TWINE BALL
FOREVER AND FOREVER
coming up short.

Good Little Hater

Couple of green WHATs?
No one gets a (bathed in peridot light)
home.

She's a singlecellanimal
on a chain
taking herself seriously
elsewhere
for
a
harmless
little
everynight screw
(now and again).

Me? One GREEN one.

Green of hat
finds
she is the NOT HIDDEN ENOUGH
link
to a meaningless sealskinned
people.

P.S. Did every cell of her body
(bathed in peridot light)
REALLY
call out to you?

The day Shirley Temple got
HERS
a woman werewolf
with jewel
            twisted
                    hair
rode the bus.
Shut the book.
The outing's an Easter Egg hunt.
WHAT WISEGUY HID MY SKIN
IN A QUAKER OATS TIN?
Luminous trails track a sky.
Luminous nails track a sky.

All in search of GODS
when bookends
came
to be sighted.

Firbank's Friend

Unpenned.
Qualmishqueer all over.
Irrevocably upset
in all but words.
Rachitic thing
carries
a baby mink gorilla.
Ouch. Hand smarts at brittle
hairs.

Firbank's friend's
noise
is a clatter of shells.
Whisper laughs
when asked to say
something
anything
IN it.

Walk-ons.
Her exit.
He enters.
Headed without an idea
to limp elegance.

Men; word-associates,
come to call.
The man with carmine-stained nails
asks after "our little inexpiable."

Joint
theories
have to do with negative ion levels
and low mold configurations
AS ART.

He loves the way she becomes
unswerved
in
shaped like hearts
moments.

The two
head
without an idea
to limp elegance.

Screw the lids on the jam glasses made in France and the world is
confident.
If I loved you in passing
no love was intended.
I'm a waste can for sperm of the moment
with a tipped lid.
Screw it
on
and the world is confident.

The glass was wrapped in tissue at the bottom of the cedar chest.
I forgot who you came after.
First pages turned by themselves with
last pages accessible to passersby.
The middle pages are stuck with Crazy Glue.
Jam is the only thing to unstuck them.

She Appeals to the Worst in Him
Portionless and Thrashing About

Peridot stone. (Our? Love.)
Finger
    placed perfectly.
Zap.
   Turns to American Flag
               embossed rice paper.
               Latin inscription reads:
               END OF THE GAME
               THE ONE WITH THE MOST TOYS
               WINS.

Full small-mouthed girls
soft red silkerly girls
lay lace and pearls at
your thrash-
        toed merman feet.
        Thrashing about.
        Sea
          pearl
             pulls thrashing toes. Pearl knack.

Lace is a yellowing emotion.
It threads mermen at dusk
where tin substitutes
old golds.
Where I come from,
Connemara is no peridot replacement.

Exponentially Speaking

RED O
O with lips
velope to the en power

Fashion models
high
for work

give peripheral glares
are
menstruating minstrels.

Now She Gets (Lucky Girl) Spending Money

My wedding.
Cry if I want to.
Yellow satin. Blood red roses. Crimson
lipstick.
Suitably depressed guests
lament on over to absinthe tents.

The ring is a large-to-huge
emerald baguette.
My Semite took one look
at me.
Sent his man digging
for a green thing.

One red and yellow girl
turns to gigglewave
after Communion.
Yuks Yuks. Makes a face.
Yuk Yuks.

TICKLISHNESSES.
Beige-suited Honeymooning Houyhnhnms
scooted off to Budapest.
Honeymoon type things followed.
Then the keeks had gone out of another
marriage.

Limits

Stingo Kink wears himself
sidesaddle
in and after a male fashion
off a motorcycle.
Certain
AWARE COMPLICATIONS DISAPPEAR WITH A DOLLAR
people
say
he's a man SPORTING SHOES.
Say
he's the author of cowboy bodice rippers.
SAY
he's got a calling.
Calling augmented
if not defined by a book
jumping on his . . .
ONTO HIS HEAD.

So long as
certain
AWARE COMPLICATIONS DISAPPEAR WITH A DOLLAR
people
say nothing
about his Mother.

O. Stingo Kink and Phroska
make the couple.
The couple gravitates to birds in the bush.
Hard weeks of HARD DAYS PEDDLING TOYS.
Bush weekends
the couple bangs hard woo woo
in abandoned wagons
beneath acid
woo woo skies.

O. Stingo
comes to her.
Comes to her longing to die.
Hard knockberries still hurt.
Spittle crusts sides of her
PROSPEROUS
PINK
PHROSKAN mouth.

Limits II

Girls on the block watch O. Stingo Kink
make his OWN lunch.
Girls are a mumbling chorus mumble
PHROSKA HAVE A CHEW ON RUBBER CEMENT mumble.
Pale slothful spitters
ain't lumpers entertaining wolfine madness.

Stingo comes to her when
confetti fills the road.
O. Stingo comes to her longing to
die.
When he comes to her.
Loves her when he comes to her.

Girls watch succubus
moonstruck Bauhaus baby PHROSKA.
Girls are thinskinned tightskinned
fresh fish.
The girls chew O.'s RUBBER CEMENT.
Phroska
no more than a hot slit
with less than a Squire's brain
said
SWEET HEROIC THINGS
RISE.
ROSE.

Stepped over locked away carvings
in order to prevent slippage.
Oil and water ways.
One or maybe two
sank
stinking
like a toothless cousin's good karma hiccup
in a dark room where broomstick
droppings
I AIN'T SHITTIN' YA
stop collapse.

In this particular RESTS ADREAM city
Shades of cheap
purplistic aperitifs
LIMIT.
The yellowest limit . . .

Li Selvaggi

Whoever
heard of not living
in the recent past?

PROPOSED TO ANYONE?
Laughs. So the red word
LAUGH
is deep in a Celtic mind
and throat.
Letter A is red
    U is deep
       covers all time.

HEADTHROWNBACKLAUGH
at ridiculousness.
Pass the Jameson's.

In-laws FIGURE
FOR WE THREE
crying shames Irish
stuck in the West Room.

We are simpatico.
You know.
The thing understood
upon impact.

Saffron.
West.
Wanton.
Weddings are for pictures.
Only one I ever wanted's
long
been taken.

Freckle-spotted Slender Neck

He placed El Greco fingers
thigh-betwixt.
Man among them.

She's Samsonite of junk
                    UNBURDENED.
HER pink stub fingers
are dusty pink neon,
fit a slender furrowed neck,
undress his
to middling excuse for an Irish tan.

What she wants?
For him to please
"not lock the door against me."

He
(fingers thigh-betwixt)
orders her to
PICK FLA$H.

God Given
Ha Ha Ha
Doldrum Name

Make me God
with no distinctions
between Miami the city
and Miami
her creatures.
Heaven Avenue is morbid gala excitement.
Open sewer Hell St.
(Luxuriously
little between.)

Little-to-no room
at the Inn
for a man   skunk-trim capped,
            Rembrandt-cloaked,
            IN A TEA GOWN.

Spell-catchers accented-German
sing "Under the Boardwalk"
IN HOPES OF A NEW MOTHER COUNTRY.

God to God
and off the record
an idea rears her ugly head.

SATISFACTION FROM A TWO-MORE-INCHES ANGLE?

Perfectly good frumps are back-walled.
Tippie toes flexed.
Breakers of face bones. (Supply and demand.)

America is where America lives
in Miami
in the mall.

Eureka
Pick up that safety pin.
Spy
on yellow-shoed girls
in the proper tweeds.

Sharpened pencil.
Stuck it in my eye.

I know I'm sane
when reminded
someone saw a sky dragon
in the year
755.

Very little color was discussed
that year.
In 755
they wore black and grey.

In the twentieth century
I stopped being mortified.

Punk is ugly
with a touch of strength.
Is ugly turning exhibitionist.
Last year you were punk.
This year you're just
plain ugly.

Degas
Boca Billy

Solidly constructed
Paris Opéra "rat"
adjusts slippers
stretches muscles.

Three violin bows. FROZE.
Black
gloved arm. FLUNG.

Pulls
dancers
dying.
Plays.

Tutued flesh
serpentines
parquet.

Frenzy.
Calm.
Not a black arm.
Glove FLUNG.
Betimes.

Red Rat's scrub hand.
Pin holding hand
WORKS
for the tailor
holds his pins.

In homely pursuit
is the blue-lensed
sketcher of the
unimportant.

Fu Man Chu Scamp Out

Though I would rather
have been,
I am not Rita Hayworth.
Not the bearded lady
with a ring in your nose.

Hug you for a crisp twenty.
Sheath's free
if you order now.
Red piece of malleable
pig iron
charred to black.

Zim zam zing zing
peas brains pings pongs heads.
Sunk the rusty dusty penny
in an army regulation dustbin.
Name backwards is forwards.
You were a nickname
they dropped next to my face.

Incarcerating creaming find,
I take you and the boots in
fuchsia.
We pass perfect plum appliances.
I continue because
stopping at the end is always
an excellent idea.